ICKY WORLD

WE NEED POO!

By Addy Farmer
Illustrated by Scott Garrett

WAYLAND

First published in Great Britain in 2023
by Wayland

Copyright © Hodder and Stoughton, 2023

Series Editor: Grace Glendinning
Series Designer: Peter Scoulding

HB ISBN: 978 1 5263 2316 3
PB ISBN: 978 1 5263 2317 0

Printed and bound in China

Wayland, an imprint of
Hachette Children's Group
Part of Hodder and Stoughton
Carmelite House
50 Victoria Embankment
London EC4Y 0DZ

An Hachette UK Company
www.hachette.co.uk
www.hachettechildrens.co.uk

MIX
Paper from
responsible sources
FSC® C104740

FSC
www.fsc.org

The website addresses (URLs) included in this book were valid at the time
of going to press. However, it is possible that contents or addresses may
have changed since the publication of this book. No responsibility for any
such changes can be accepted by either the author or the Publisher.

CONTENTS

What on Earth is POO?

**Faeces, excrement, dung, stools, scat —
there are so many different words for poo!**

**But what *IS* it? And why do scatologists (scientists
who study poo) think it's so fascinating?**

POO-EE!

Poo is the waste bits of food an animal can't
digest, such as seeds and fibre, all mixed up
with water, bacteria and slimy mucus.

All animals do poos, from the tiniest speck of
fly poo to the blue whale's huge plume of poo
(which can stretch up to 20 m long).

People poo

Let's not forget about human poo! Humans across Earth altogether poo about 290 billion kg per year. Add in all the other animal poo, and it can lead to a whole heap of poo problems, from disease to pollution.

All this poo has got to go somewhere!

So, what we do with our poo matters.

Eat, poo, renew!

In this book, we'll learn from amazing animals who eat, poo and renew in habitats across the world.

We'll also see how poo can do vital work in keeping the world's ecosystems in balance.

Yes, poo can be smelly and gross – nature's way of keeping us away from potential disease – but it can also be useful, from farming to building.

Poo is information!

Scientists who study prehistoric poos, which are called coprolites, have made lots of important discoveries about how animals lived millions of years ago.

Big dinosaurs did big poos! The **Argentinosaurus** ate lots of plants and pooed out more than 20 kg at a time.

What dino ate for dinner

Poke about in a coprolite and you may find bits of bone, teeth and claws. This dino was definitely a meat-eater!

About 75 million years ago the **Hadrosaurus** that pooed this out grazed on leaves, wood and fungi.

Dino poo ecosystem

All that dinosaur poo was a source of food for smaller animals and insects, and for bacteria (see pages 14-15 for how animals today eat poo, too). And the poo played an important part in making Earth's early soil a healthy mix for early plant life.

Dino poo and its poo-eating friends helped keep prehistoric vegetation lush and green by adding nutrients back into the soil.

Creature shout-out: DUNG BEETLE

There are thousands of different types of dung beetle found on every continent (except Antarctica), and each is a poo pro! They are specially skilled **decomposers**.

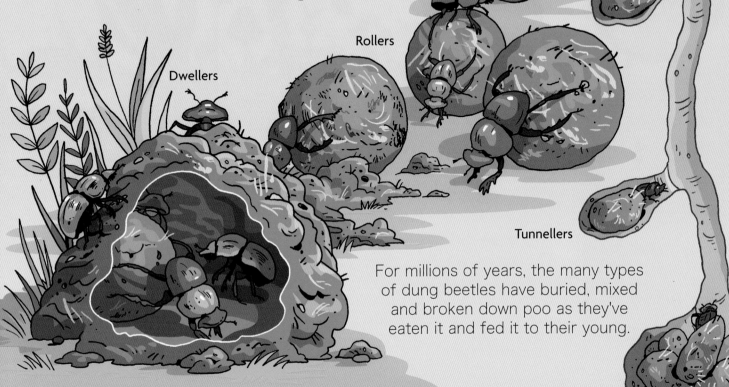

Dwellers

Rollers

Tunnellers

For millions of years, the many types of dung beetles have buried, mixed and broken down poo as they've eaten it and fed it to their young.

7

plants love poo

How do the world's plants grow?
With the help of poo!

Fantastic fertiliser

Animal poo all over the world today acts as a fertiliser for Earth's soil. This helps plants grow faster and stronger. How does this work?

Bacteria at work

Slimy bacteria, insects, fungi and other decomposers dive in and break down the poo, including any harmful bits. They are eco heroes!

Plants then absorb nutrients from the decomposed poo that they can't get from the air. These include nitrogen, phosphorus and potassium.

Poo on the farm

Farmers also use livestock poo to grow crops for us to eat.

Animal poo can be spread over fields as solid manure, as compost (poo mixed with other natural waste) or as slurry (liquified animal poo sprayed by machine).

Solid manure   Compost mix

Slurry spray

Poo in the loo

Some farmers have found a way to make good use of all the human-made poo, too.

To make it safe for using on food crops, human poo has to be composted. It gets mixed up with plant waste, and then helpful microbes work away, which kills harmful bacteria.

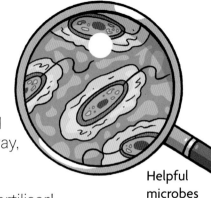

Helpful microbes

What's left is a safe and rich fertiliser!

Poo in the oceans

Sea-pooers help to maintain the health of the world's oceans.

Sea cucumbers suck up sand, filter out the waste, then poo out cleaner sand. This means that fish can breathe more easily and that seagrasses, corals and shellfish can thrive on a healthy ocean floor.

Sea cucumber pooing

Parrotfish eat slimy algae off coral reefs and poo it out as sand. (Walk on the famous white-sand beaches of Hawaii and you're walking on parrotfish poo!)

Parrotfish pooing

Here's the biggy!

Whale poo is like a global fertiliser. Mineral-rich whale poo feeds the ocean's plants and animals, and even humans – it's an eco poop loop!

1 Whales deposit iron-rich poo near the ocean's surface.

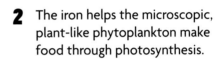

2 The iron helps the microscopic, plant-like phytoplankton make food through photosynthesis.

3 Lots of healthy phytoplankton means zooplankton – animal plankton, such as krill and copepods – can be well-fed and thrive, too!

4 Plankton feeds many sea animals, including small fish (and the not-so-small whales)!

5 Small fish feed large fish.

6 Seabirds (and humans!) eat fish and then poo out nutrients on land.

The poo that just keeps giving

Healthy ocean plants suck in more than half of the world's carbon dioxide (CO_2), which helps our climate stay cool. They couldn't do it without whale poo!

posting poo

Animal poo is used as a travel service for plants to send their seeds far and wide. It's also a nutritious delivery for some clever carnivorous plants.

Poo builds biodiversity: in the sea, on land and up in the trees!

The **tambaqui**, also known as the vegetarian piranha, eats fruit that has fallen into the water from the trees of the Amazon rainforest. It eventually poos out the seeds, where currents can carry it up to 5 km away.

Birds such as **robins** and **thrushes** love to eat mistletoe berries. As they pass through the birds, the mistletoe seeds get super-sticky. This means they can cling to the next tree they land on as poo.

The new mistletoe plant will sprout from cracks in the bark where they land.

Bears eat lots of fruit. The seeds grow into plants in new places, and the plant growth is helped along by the poo fertiliser at the same time.

Make a deposit, please

Pitcher plants in South America have specially shaped leaves that bounce back **bat** squeaks, attracting bats to come, sit, eat and poo! The poo is a source of food for the plant.

Another type of pitcher plant makes sugary secretions to lure in **tree shrews** and **rats**, who then leave some poo-ey goodness behind.

Poo as the animals do

What do animals do with all their poo?

Many baby animals, such as **elephants** or **hippo** calves, eat their mums' poo! It introduces healthy gut microbes for digesting tough-to-eat leaves.

The poo web: it's not just for baby elephants

A poo feast feeds into many ecosystems!

The insects attract insect-eating amphibians, such as frogs ...

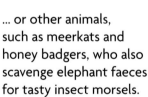

... or other animals, such as meerkats and honey badgers, who also scavenge elephant faeces for tasty insect morsels.

Elephants eat lots of leaves and do a lot of big poos!

Along come the dung beetles and other decomposer insects.

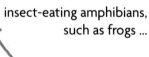

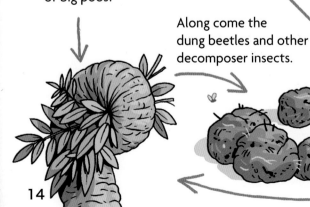

Whatever is left over goes into the soil to help plants grow lots of delicious leaves ... for the elephants to eat!

Herbivores, such as **zebras** and **cows**, leave one third of the nutrients they get from their food in their poo. They eat it again to get all the bits missed the first time.

The **southern cassowary** eats cassowary plums, which are barely digested the first time. They come out as yummy chunks of fruit. Tuck in again!

Guinea pigs and **rabbits** occasionally do especially nutritious poos called cecotropes. They often eat them straight from their own bottoms. Yum bum!

Poo prey or poo predator?

Animals use poo to fight, hide or even as a disguise.

Brazilian skipper butterfly larvae (3.8 cm long) can shoot their faeces, called frass, up to 2 m away. Stay away!

Hoopoe chicks can squirt a jet of poo, which they aim right at the eyes of potential predators.

Hoopoe chick shooting poo from its nest

Brazilian skipper caterpillar sends out a poo missile

Ballistic poo

Throughout history, even humans have used poo as a weapon to fling at enemies – much like our **ape** relatives still do today!

Sneaky poo disguise

Lions, wolves and **jackals** roll in strong-smelling poo to mask their scents, so they can sneak up on their prey.

Poo can be a lifesaver!

The **pygmy sperm whale** hides from its enemies in its own cloud of poo.

Dung spiders and some **caterpillars** have evolved to *look like* poo to ward off predators.

> POO HOO!
> Where are you?

EW!

The **potato beetle** covers itself in toxic poo to avoid being eaten.

Poo news

Poo can be an important method of communication for wildlife.

Marking territory

"Clear off! This is my place!" Sometimes poo sends a very strong message about where an animal has claimed its home.

Wombats spread their square-shaped poo around their territory each day to warn others away.

Some species of **rhino** do similar, but they go one step further: they shuffle their back feet in the poo so everywhere they walk leaves a scent trail.

Find your way by poo

The **hippo** leaves a trail of dung to find its way back home.

Poo chats

Pooing leaves a strong and unique scent, which can be a positive thing, too.

Two-toed sloths create poo heaps, called dung middens, to establish mating sites for themselves and for the moths that live in their coats. How generous!

Some creatures, such as **genets** and **lemurs**, create 'toilets' in a raised area, and leave messages for relatives and potential mates in this central, protected location.

Giant otters build community toilets, too – on river banks.

Otter groups hang out in the toilet a lot, learning important information about each other from their poos, and marking their group's territory for passing rivals.

POO PARTY!

Poo homes

Some animals will live in whatever poo they think will make a good home.

The **secretary bird** uses zebra poo to stick together its nest.

Oven birds make mud nests, but will also use antelope poo when mud is in short supply.

Millipedes make a nest for their eggs from tiny poo bricks left behind by insects.

Special mention: cuckoo spit! While it's not strictly poo, it does come out of the **froghopper nymph's** bottom. These nymphs blow air through a liquid to create foam (all with their bums), so that they can hide inside it from predators.

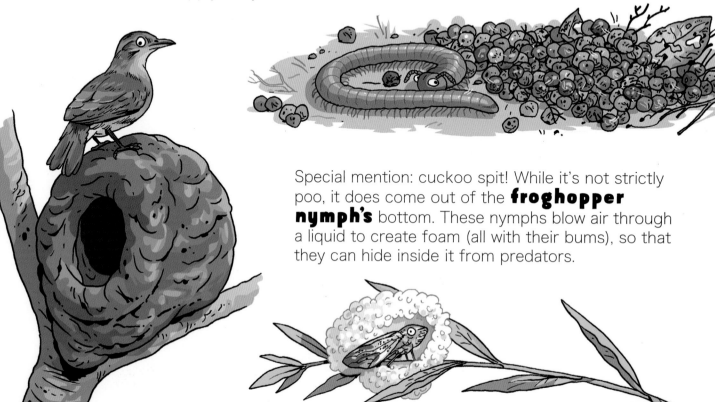

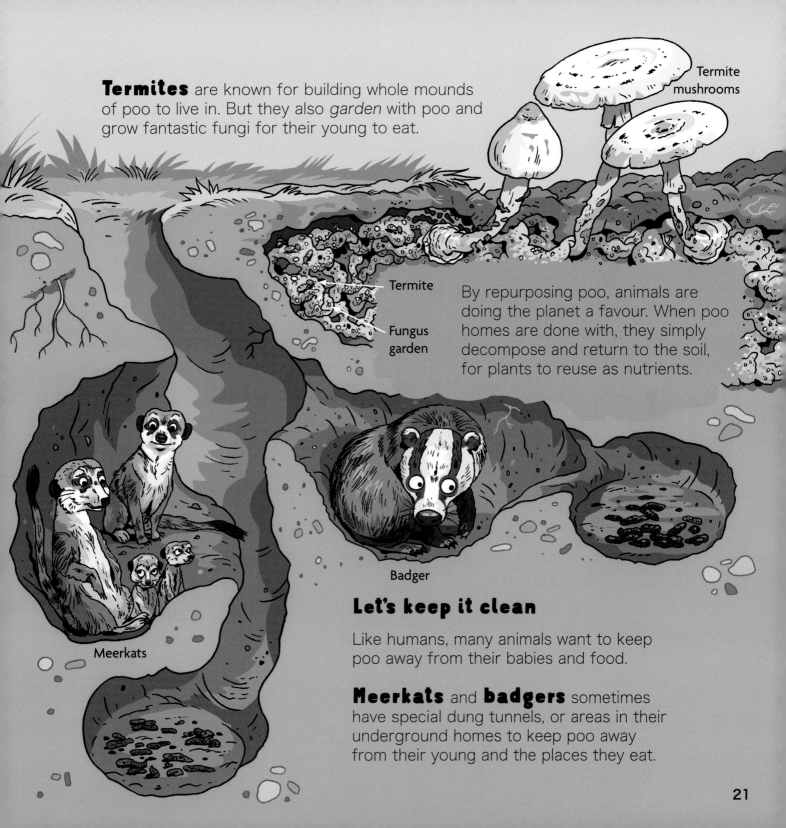

Termites are known for building whole mounds of poo to live in. But they also *garden* with poo and grow fantastic fungi for their young to eat.

Termite mushrooms

Termite

Fungus garden

By repurposing poo, animals are doing the planet a favour. When poo homes are done with, they simply decompose and return to the soil, for plants to reuse as nutrients.

Meerkats

Badger

Let's keep it clean

Like humans, many animals want to keep poo away from their babies and food.

Meerkats and **badgers** sometimes have special dung tunnels, or areas in their underground homes to keep poo away from their young and the places they eat.

21

Humans use poo, too

Humans tend to think of poo as smelly and disgusting but, like other animals, we have used it in all sorts of ways!

We want your poo

Throughout history, bird poo called guano has been collected as a valuable fertiliser, and for use in weaponry. There was even a war fought over it.

1860s: Chile, Peru and Spain fought a war over possession of the guano-covered Chincha Islands.

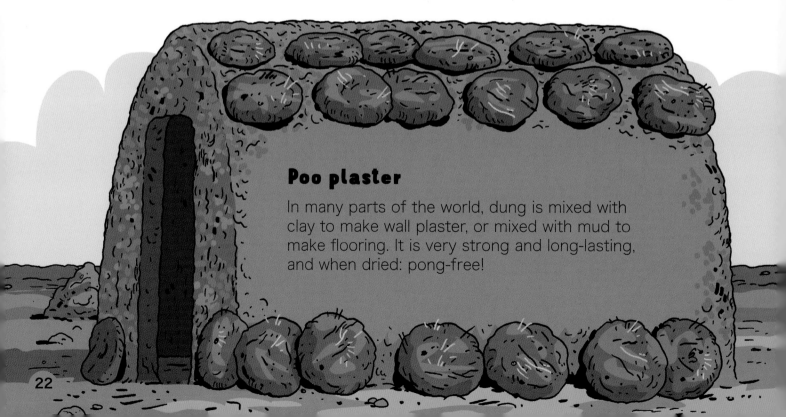

Poo plaster

In many parts of the world, dung is mixed with clay to make wall plaster, or mixed with mud to make flooring. It is very strong and long-lasting, and when dried: pong-free!

Poo food

Many delicacies can be enjoyed thanks to poo. Lots of people drink coffee made from coffee beans pooed out by a civet, or tea leaves pooed out by a caterpillar.

And a limited-edition batch of elephant-poo-coffee-flavoured beer sold out quickly to many eager customers.

Civet poo

Elephant poo

Grain moth larvae poo

Powered by poo

Scientists have developed machines called biodigesters, which break down poo and create a fuel called biogas. This can be used to light and heat up homes, cars and buses.

Energy made from the animal poo at Canada's Toronto Zoo feeds right into the city's electricity supply. In the UK, one inventor figured out a way to use dog poo energy to keep street lights running!

Poo renews all day long

Poo possibilities are endless! It's been converted into biodegradable plastics, water filters and even paper. And because poo is inescapable, it's a highly renewable resource.

Bioplastic bottle

Llama poo water filter

Elephant poo paper

Poo problems

Too much poo can pollute the environment and also cause disease. Humans must deal with our poo wisely to avoid disaster.

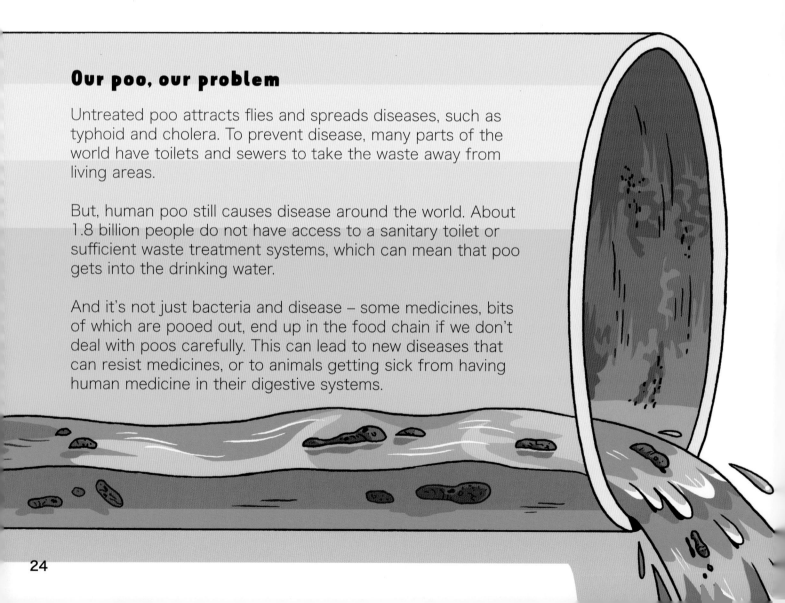

Our poo, our problem

Untreated poo attracts flies and spreads diseases, such as typhoid and cholera. To prevent disease, many parts of the world have toilets and sewers to take the waste away from living areas.

But, human poo still causes disease around the world. About 1.8 billion people do not have access to a sanitary toilet or sufficient waste treatment systems, which can mean that poo gets into the drinking water.

And it's not just bacteria and disease – some medicines, bits of which are pooed out, end up in the food chain if we don't deal with poos carefully. This can lead to new diseases that can resist medicines, or to animals getting sick from having human medicine in their digestive systems.

Dung can bung up the atmosphere and rivers

The world's livestock produces billions of tonnes of poo every year. Methane gas from all the decaying poo is a significant cause of climate change.

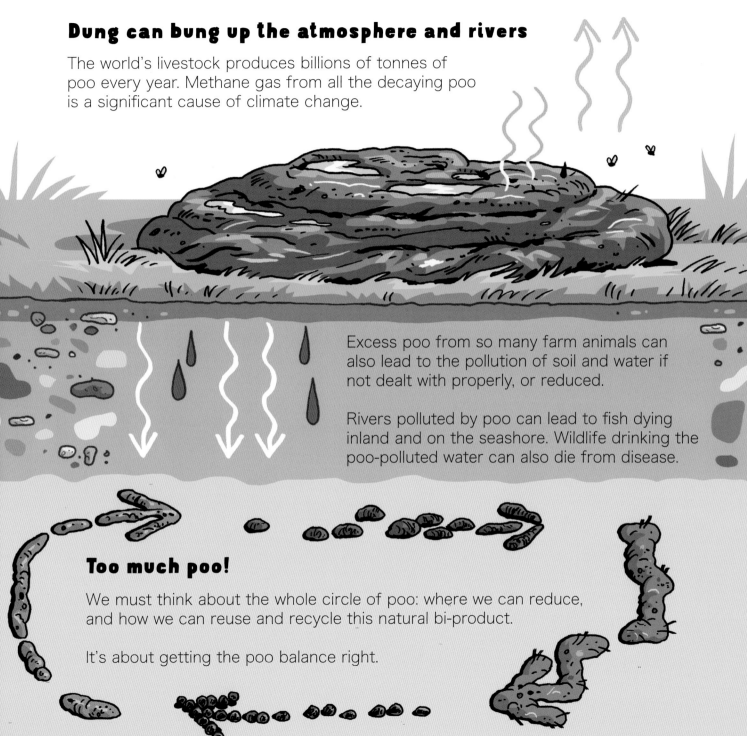

Excess poo from so many farm animals can also lead to the pollution of soil and water if not dealt with properly, or reduced.

Rivers polluted by poo can lead to fish dying inland and on the seashore. Wildlife drinking the poo-polluted water can also die from disease.

Too much poo!

We must think about the whole circle of poo: where we can reduce, and how we can reuse and recycle this natural bi-product.

It's about getting the poo balance right.

Poo protection: what can be dung?

Poo is everywhere on Earth! Let's talk about lots of different ways to work with poo.

Poo food for thought

Around the world, people are thinking about how to recycle more poo as a **sustainable fertiliser**. As a fertiliser, poo can continue to help feed living things, without piling up.

Creating **less poo overall** is also a helpful way forward! For example, eating less meat cuts down on the amount of animals that are farmed, and the mountains of poo they make.

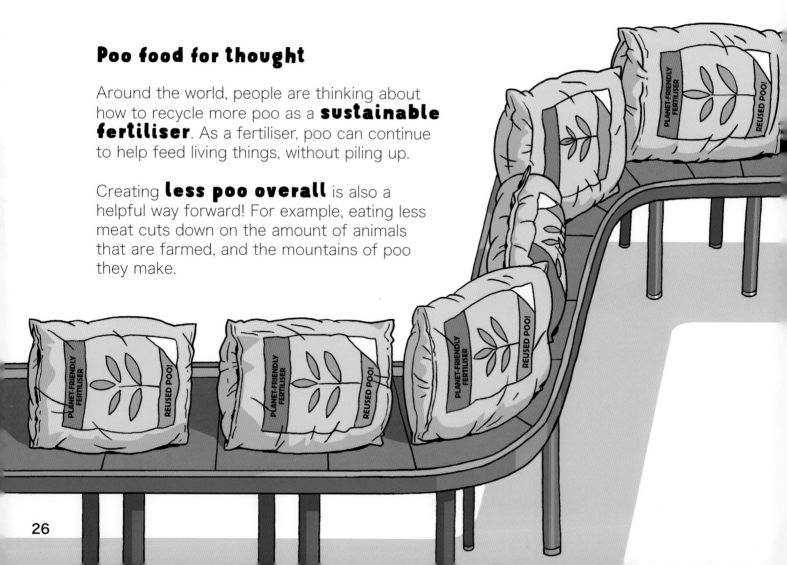

Poo friends

Poo needs help! By working with nature, and using **fewer chemicals**, lots of farmers and industries are helping to maintain all those poo-munching heroes, such as the dung beetle.

Leaving our decomposers to safely deal with the poo means less of the methane that adds to climate change.

Poo is power!

It's not just your poo in the loo. The way we **process** and **treat** poo affects the planet's ecosystems and our future.

NO DUMPING!

KEEP OUR RIVERS CLEAN!

USE THE POOS!

What you can do ...

Poo the right thing!

Remember to flush only poo, pee and paper. By keeping the sewers full of only biodegradable materials, you're helping bacteria to get working to process that poo.

Be a scatologist

How about an owl-pellet hunt? Get to know the animals in your local area through this amazing source of scientific information.

WITH PERMISSION and HELP FROM AN ADULT:

- Look for owl pellets at the base of tall trees, or perhaps on the floor of a barn where you've seen barn owls fly.
- Note the size, shape and colour on a piece of paper.
- Break it apart with a stick and see what's inside. You might see lots of tiny bones from its prey!
- Report your findings to a local conservation group or prepare a poster for your classmates!

... for poo!

Be more like the dung beetle

Poo and renew! Perhaps you can find out about a local poo-composting project, or start your own with the help of an adult? Inform and inspire others to do what's best with this never-ending resource.

Keep talking about poo!

WARNING: Poo is great stuff, but **never** handle it with bare hands or without adult supervision, and **always** be sure to wash your hands if you have been **anywhere** around it!

Glossary

Bacteria – one-celled living things of which there are many, many species. Some species of bacteria can cause disease, while others do not.

Biodiversity – all the variety of life, whether plants, animals, fungi or microorganisms, as well as the ecosystems they form and the habitats in which they live.

Carnivore – an animal that mostly eats other animals.

Climate change (global warming) – the process of our planet heating up and our world weather changing. This is due to many reasons, including methane escaping into the atmosphere. For example, methane is released as livestock dung breaks down.

Compost – decayed, organic material used as a fertiliser for growing plants.

Decomposers – something that breaks down materials into simpler substances

Ecosystem – all the organisms living in a certain area, and how they interact with that environment to form a natural community.

Fertiliser – a substance containing nutrients that plants need to grow. Fertiliser can be organic (poo) or synthetic (made artificially by scientists through a chemical process).

Fibre – a type of carbohydrate found in foods, such as wholegrains, beans, fruit and vegetables, which the body can't digest. It helps your food to move through your digestive system.

Greenhouse gas – gases in Earth's atmosphere that trap heat and keep the Earth warm. Too much of these gases, such as methane or carbon dioxide, means the Earth heats up too much.

Habitat – the home environment for plants and animals or other organisms. Examples of habitats include: desert, meadow and woodland.

Herbivore – animals that only eat plants.

Microbes – the tiny living microorganisms you cannot see with the naked eye, for example bacteria and viruses.

Microbiome – the group of good microbes inside our guts, which keep our bodies healthy.

Nutrients – any substance that plants, animals or fungi need in order to live and grow.

Nymph – the young of some insects

Phytoplankton – a type of algae that provides food for a range of animals in freshwater and the oceans.

Pollutant – any substance that makes soil, water or air dirty and unhealthy, such as raw sewage or plastic.

Zooplankton – very small animals, such as water mites and crustaceans, that float near the surface of water and provide food for other animals.

Further info

Find out more about the icky bits of nature!

Books:

The *Animals Do* series
by Paul Mason, Tony De Saulles & Gemma Hastilow, Wayland 2018–20
The Poo That Animals Do, The Wee That Animals Pee
The Farts That Animals Parp, The Snot That Animals Have Got

The Poo-niverse
by Paul Mason and Fran Bueno, Wayland 2020

The *Outdoor Science* series
by Sonya Newland & Izzi Howell, Wayland 2018–19

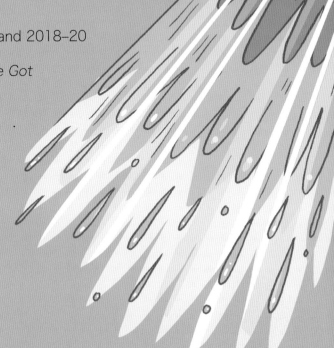

Websites:

https://www.bbc.co.uk/gardening/gardening_with_
children/homegrownprojects_compost.shtml
to find out about composting safely as a family

www.natgeokids.com/uk/dirtisgoodacademy
to help make a difference for our icky world

www.nhm.ac.uk/discover/what-is-a-coprolite.html
to learn more about dinosaur poos

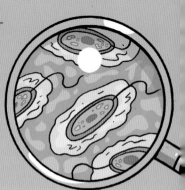

INDEX